GOOD BOOKS, GOOD TIMES!

selected by Lee Bennett Hopkins

pictures by Harvey Stevenson

A Charlotte Zolotow Book

An Imprint of HarperCollins*Publishers*

To Myra Cohn Livingston
for
"the untold mystery"
LBH

GOOD BOOKS, GOOD TIMES!
Text copyright © 1990 by Lee Bennett Hopkins
Illustrations copyright © 1990 by Harvey Stevenson
Manufactured in China. All rights reserved.

Library of Congress Cataloging-in-Publication Data
Good books, good times! : poems / selected by Lee Bennett Hopkins ;
    illustrated by Harvey Stevenson.
        p.   cm.
    "A Charlotte Zolotow book."
    Summary: An anthology of poems about the joys of books and
reading. Includes selections by David McCord, Karla Kuskin, Myra
Cohn Livingston, and Jack Prelutsky.
    ISBN 0-06-022528-9 (lib. bdg.) — ISBN 0-06-446222-6 (pbk.)
    1. Books and reading—Juvenile poetry.   2. Children's poetry,
American.   [1. Books and reading—Poetry.   2. American poetry—
Collections.]   I. Hopkins, Lee Bennett.   II. Stevenson, Harvey, ill.
PS595.B65G66   1990   89-49108
811'.54080357—dc20   CIP
                                                                       AC

Visit us on the World Wide Web!
http://www.harperchildrens.com

ACKNOWLEDGMENTS

Grateful acknowledgment is made to the following,
whose work appears in this volume:

William Cole for "Summer Doings." Copyright by William Cole. By permission of the author, who controls all rights.

Curtis Brown, Ltd., for "Good Books, Good Times!" by Lee Bennett Hopkins. Copyright © 1985 by Lee Bennett Hopkins. Reprinted by permission of Curtis Brown, Ltd.

Teaching Pre K-8 for the poem beginning "There is a land" by Leland B. Jacobs, from the November/December 1985 issue of *Early Years/K-8*. Reprinted by permission of the publisher, Teaching Pre K-8, Westport, Connecticut 06880.

Aileen Fisher for the poem beginning "On a day in summer." Children's Book Council, 1981. By permission of the author, who controls all rights.

Isabel Joshlin Glaser for "What If...." Used by permission of the author, who controls all rights.

Greenwillow Books for "Books to the Ceiling," from *Whiskers and Rhymes* by Arnold Lobel. Copyright © 1985 by Arnold Lobel. By permission of Greenwillow Books (A Division of William Morrow).

William J. Harris for "An Historic Moment." Used by permission of the author, who controls all rights.

X. J. Kennedy for the poem beginning, "I'd like a story of." By permission of X. J. Kennedy, who controls all rights. First published on a bookmark distributed by Children's Book Council.

Karla Kuskin for "Being Lost." Poem for Children's Book Council. Copyright © 1975 by Karla Kuskin. Reprinted by permission of the author, who controls all rights.

Little, Brown and Company, for "Books Fall Open" from *One at a Time* by David McCord. Copyright © 1965, 1966 by David McCord. By permission of Little, Brown and Company.

Beverly McLoughland for "Surprise." Reprinted by permission of the author, who controls all rights. Originally appeared in *Cricket* magazine, 1985.

Jack Prelutsky for "I Met a Dragon Face to Face." Copyright © 1986 by Jack Prelutsky. Reprinted by permission of the author, who controls all rights.

Prince Redcloud for "And Then." Used by permission of the author, who controls all rights.

Marian Reiner for "Give Me A Book" from *4-Way Stop and Other Poems* by Myra Cohn Livingston. Copyright © 1976 by Myra Cohn Livingston. Reprinted by permission of Marian Reiner for the author.

4

BEING LOST

Being lost
Is the perfect way
To pass the time
On a sky blue day

When it's warm
And the open window
Uncurtains a call
Spiraling up the stairway
Hovering in the hall.
No one comes then
When they call me.
I am not there
Where they look.
I linger alone
In a place of my own
Lost
In a book.

Karla Kuskin

BOOKS FALL OPEN

Books fall open,
you fall in,
delighted where
you've never been;
hear voices not once
heard before,
reach world on world
through door on door;
find unexpected
keys to things
locked up beyond
imaginings.
What *might* you be,
perhaps *become*,

because one book
is somewhere? Some
wise delver into
wisdom, wit,
and wherewithal
has written it.
True books will venture,
dare you out,
whisper secrets,
maybe shout
across the gloom
to you in need,
who hanker for
a book to read.

David McCord

AND THEN

I was reading
a poem
about snow

when
the sun
came out
and
melted it.

Prince Redcloud

ON A DAY IN SUMMER

On a day in summer
where the path made a crook
a boy leaned on a boulder
and opened a book.

He didn't hear the cricket
on the meadow's floor,
he didn't hear the fledglings
begging, "More, more, more."

He didn't feel the shadow
sliding down the tree,
he didn't see the closeness
of a bumblebee.

He didn't see the rabbit
or smell the yellow clover...
he wasn't even *hungry*
till the book was over.

Aileen Fisher

GIVE ME A BOOK

Give me a book
   and long tall grass,
There will I look
   as the hours pass

To other places
   I can see;
To other faces
   strange to me.

In black and white
   they fill my head
With men and women—
   vanished, dead—

Of hope and fear,
   of wish and need.
The world stands still.
   I, breathless, read,

And in their history
   I see
The untold mystery
   Of me.

Myra Cohn Livingston

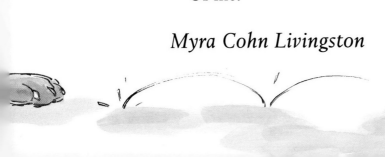

SUMMER DOINGS

Some at beaches
   Are sand-castling;
Some are silly—
   Fighting, rasseling!

Some are swimming,
   Camping, hiking;
Some say stickball
   Is their liking.

Some on bikes are
   Gaily speeding;
Some are smarter—

   SUMMER READING!

William Cole

15

GOOD BOOKS, GOOD TIMES!

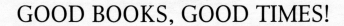

Good books.
Good times.
Good stories.
Good rhymes.
Good beginnings.
Good ends.
Good people.
Good friends.
Good fiction.
Good facts.
Good adventures.
Good acts.
Good stories.
Good rhymes.
Good books.
Good times.

Lee Bennett Hopkins

AN HISTORIC MOMENT

The man said,
after inventing poetry,
"WOW!"
and did a full somersault.

William J. Harris

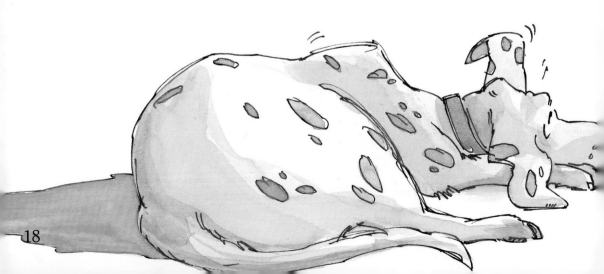

WHAT IF…

What if…
   You opened a book
   About dinosaurs
And one stumbled out
And another and another
   And more and more pour
Until the whole place
Is bumbling and rumbling
And groaning and moaning
   And snoring and roaring
And dinosauring?

What if…
   You tried to push them
   Back inside
But they kept tromping
Off the pages instead?
   Would you close the covers?

Isabel Joshlin Glaser

I MET A DRAGON
FACE TO FACE

I met a dragon face to face
the year when I was ten,
I took a trip to outer space,
I braved a pirates' den,
I wrestled with a wicked troll,
and fought a great white shark,
I trailed a rabbit down a hole,
I hunted for a snark.

I stowed aboard a submarine,
I opened magic doors,
I traveled in a time machine,
and searched for dinosaurs,
I climbed atop a giant's head,
I found a pot of gold,
I did all this in books I read
when I was ten years old.

Jack Prelutsky

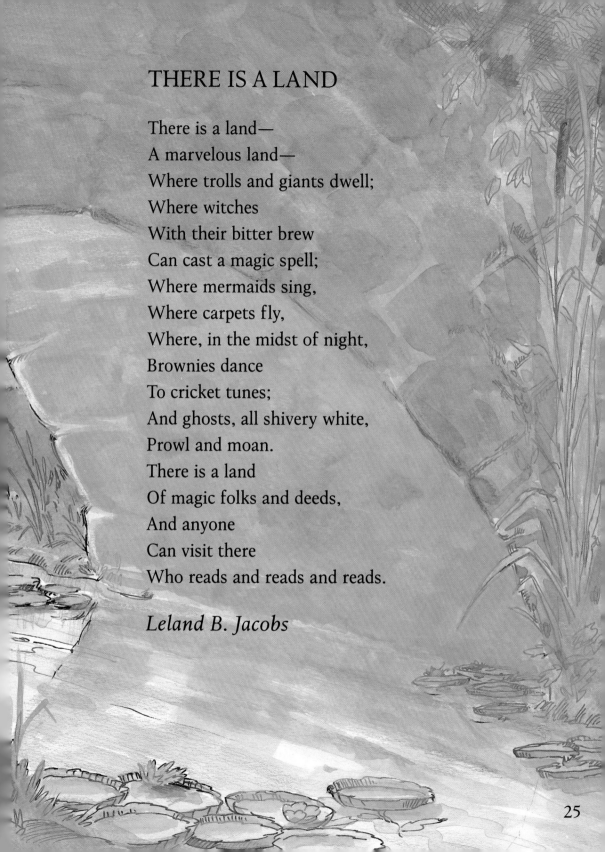

THERE IS A LAND

There is a land—
A marvelous land—
Where trolls and giants dwell;
Where witches
With their bitter brew
Can cast a magic spell;
Where mermaids sing,
Where carpets fly,
Where, in the midst of night,
Brownies dance
To cricket tunes;
And ghosts, all shivery white,
Prowl and moan.
There is a land
Of magic folks and deeds,
And anyone
Can visit there
Who reads and reads and reads.

Leland B. Jacobs

I'D LIKE A STORY

I'd like a story of
Ghosts on gusty nights,
Wild island ponies galloping
With manes that wave like kites,
A book that knows the lowdown
On what to feed giraffes,
A book of nutty nonsense
That's nothing much—just laughs—

A book to read to find out
How basketball stars shoot,
Why dinosaurs all died out,
What do computers compute,
Which sail a mizzen sail is,
Can Martians really be,
How heavy a blue whale is,
Weighed side by side with me—

A book to curl in bed with,
To browse in by a brook—
Anytime!

    Anyplace!
I'd like any book!

X. J. Kennedy

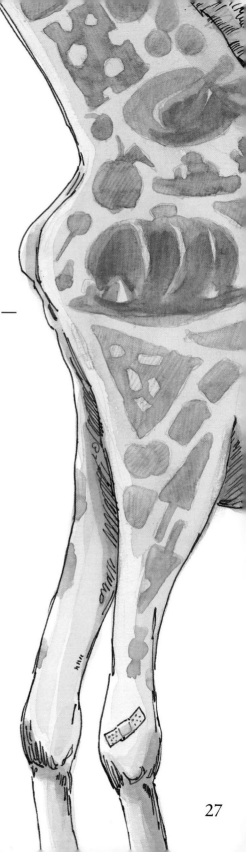

BOOKS TO THE CEILING

Books to the ceiling, books to the sky.
My piles of books are a mile high.
How I love them!
How I need them!
I'll have a long beard by the time I read them.

Arnold Lobel

SURPRISE

The biggest
Surprise
On the library shelf
Is when you suddenly
Find yourself
Inside a book—
(The *hidden* you)

You wonder how
The author knew.

Beverly McLoughland

31

INDEX OF AUTHORS AND TITLES

And Then, 9

Being Lost, 5
Books Fall Open, 6
Books to the Ceiling, 29

Cole, William, 14

Fisher, Aileen, 10

Give Me a Book, 13
Glaser, Isabel Joshlin, 21
Good Books, Good Times!, 17

Harris, William J., 18
Historic Moment, An, 18
Hopkins, Lee Bennett, 17

I'd Like a Story, 27
I Met a Dragon Face to Face, 22

Jacobs, Leland B., 25

Kennedy, X. J., 27
Kuskin, Karla, 5

Livingston, Myra Cohn, 13
Lobel, Arnold, 29

McCord, David, 6
McLoughland, Beverly, 30

On a Day in Summer, 10

Prelutsky, Jack, 22

Redcloud, Prince, 9

Summer Doings, 14
Surprise, 30

There Is a Land, 25

What if..., 21